How to Create LSMW Programs

How to for SAP Legacy System Migration Workbench

By Lawrence Compagna, C.P.A.

Second edition copyright 2017 by the Candco Corporation.

ISBN: 978-1-947618-00-8

Published by the Candco Corporation

*Dedicated to my mother for encouraging me,
Madison for showing me how to be creative,
Conrad for the intellectual stimulation, and finally
to Wyatt ... who forever inspires me*

How to Create LSMW Programs

Table of Contents

Preface and Background

This booklet is an expanded version of an earlier document I published called "Easily Create Your Own LSMW Data Load Program in SAP". From that earlier work I have elaborated on the creation process, and added a new section with step-by-step instructions showing you how to run your LSMW. As always I welcome your comments and input on improving this document on my Facebook page devoted to the subject and titled "SAP LSMW".

SAP is a German software package used extensively by the world's largest organizations for accounting, financial control, production control, human resources, material management planning, and many other facets of business' operation. For those readers who do not know SAP stands for "Systems, Applications and Processes in data processing". The core of the solution, ECC, stands for the "Enterprise Central Component". The predecessor of the Enterprise Central Component was R/3, and before that it was R/2. The origins of the SAP ERP system date back to 1972 when it was founded as a mainframe software system. In 1992 they developed their client server based ERP program and their growth has exploded since then.

The hallmark of SAP is the tight integration of its core business suite. This core product is based on industry best practices. Consequently SAP is the world's leading ERP software manufacturer.

This book assumes that the reader has a good understanding of the SAP ECC (Enterprise Central

Component) system and is either a consultant on an implementation or an active super user of the software.

When I use the term partner, implementation partner, consultant, consulting firm, advisor, integrator, or systems integrator all of these terms should be considered synonymous. All of these terms refer to a third party firm hired to assist an organization which has a license for SAP in making changes to it or using it.

When I use the term "the business", I am referring to any organization (both private and public sector) that is having SAP implemented, modified, or upgraded within it. This term will never be used to denote the implementation partner that is advising and assisting "the business" with their implementation. The implementation partner will be referred to with that term, or as a similar term such partner, advisor, or integrator.

Furthermore the term "implementation" will be used to denote any major SAP project (with an arbitrary budget of over $1 million), that could in fact be a re-implementation, enhancement project, module deployment, the end-to-end deployment of an entire new business process, or an upgrade.

When I use the term "super user" I am referring to a member of the "business" who displays superior acumen for using the SAP system and who has been given the authorization to use a tool like the Legacy System Migration Workbench, also known as LSMW.

This book also assumes that the reader has access to an SAP test system so as to follow along with the instructions shown.

Caution: do not practice LSMW techniques in a productive system.

Introduction

If you've ever been involved with SAP, either as a consultant or as a user, you've inevitably encountered the need to load large amounts of data to the system. By large, I mean hundreds or thousands of records. The numbers are so large that manually keying them in is impractical unless you have a staff of data entry clerks. Even if you had such a staff, wouldn't it be nice to simply have a tool to load the records yourself?

That's what LSMW is. The Legacy System Migration Workbench is a tool that allows a non-programmer to load large amounts of data into the system. Hundreds, thousands, or even tens of thousands of records can be loaded into SAP at a rate on the order of 5,000 per hour.

In this book you will learn how to use Legacy System Migration Workbench (LSMW) to assist your data conversion.

The tool itself is relatively simple to use, with no coding required. As we shall see creating an LSMW is tantamount to recording a macro using a front end transaction. The starting point is to decide on the actual transaction code that you intend to base your program on. For example, if you intend to create a program to load general ledger account master data record base your program on a transaction such as FS00.

How to Create LSMW Programs

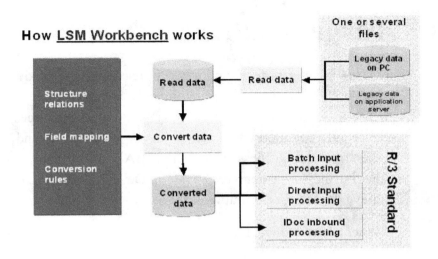

Target Audience

This book is meant for functional people (consultants and super-users) as opposed to developers. Developers have their own toolbox that includes LSMW and other resources that require coding. Functional people are people who tend to be "from the business" side, with MBA's, CPA's, and other business type degrees prevalent. Developers will tend to have degrees in computing science.

As mentioned earlier, functional people will be either consultants from an implementation partner, or "super-users" from the business. In a live environment it is likely that the use of LSMW will entail special security privileges that only a super user would be given.

Purpose

The purpose of this book is to give functional people –
consultants and super users - a tool to load large amounts of
data into SAP without the involvement of a developer. By
large I mean up to 100,000 records. Anything larger than
that may exceed the capabilities of this macro type of
LSMW and may require the involvement of a developer.

In change mode click on Batch input recording and click on overview 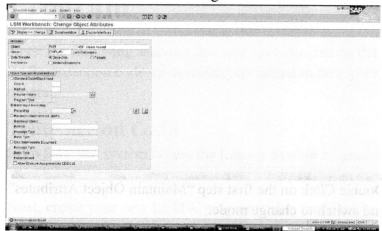 next to recording:

Click on the blank page icon and give it a name and description (at least four characters required).

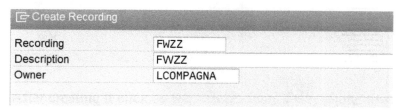

In the next screen enter the transaction code which will be used to record your macro.

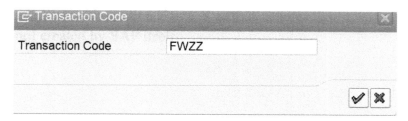

16

Click on the green check mark or hit enter to begin
recording. The screen will look familiar to you as it is
simply the native transaction code and looks no different
than it does in normal circumstances. Enter the values you
want to upload. If a field is populated, but you want to
ensure it as part of the load program you are building, then
click on it (you don't need to change it).

After saving the transaction you get the screen shown
below. Click on each of the highlighted fields and add a
name and description. If it is not part of the program delete
it using delete screen field (for example I deleted
Ra02s_nassets because it was just "number of assets" to
create and it was not relevant to my situation). If you don't
want a default, clear that field.

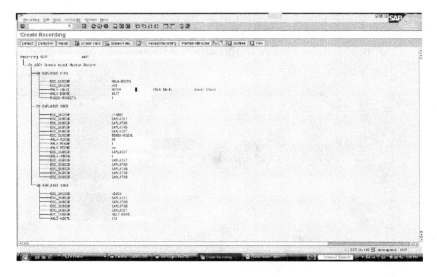

Save and exit until you get back to the screen where the
recording was kicked off and enter the new recording name

that you created earlier into the field for "recording" and save.

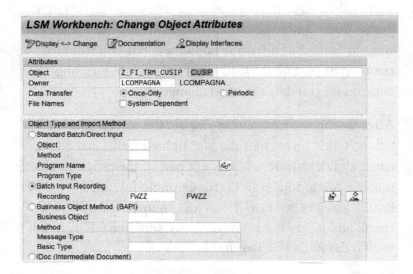

After saving you get back to the screen below. Click on Source structures, switch to change mode, and click on the blank piece of paper to create an object. Give it any name.

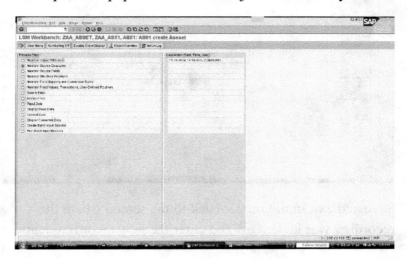

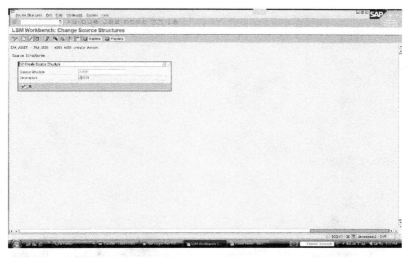

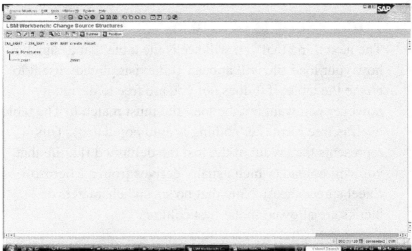

Save and backup. Click on the next item (you will be moved there automatically by SAP). Switch to change mode and then click on table maintenance in the screen below:

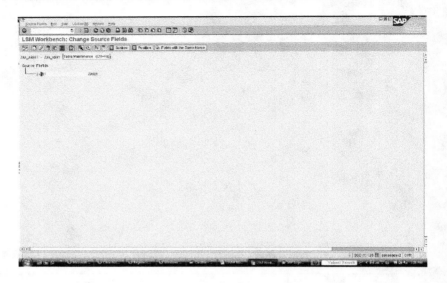

File Layout (For Import)

The next thing that you will see is the table that designates how your load file will appear. If it exists already use it to create the table; if it does not you are free to design it however you want but the load file must match it. The table itself is free form (i.e. nothing is auto populated). This represents the layout of the text tab delimited flat file that you will upload (which usually derives from a Microsoft Excel spreadsheet). Note that no special characters or blanks are allowed in the first column.

Save and exit. This will move you automatically to the next step in the LSMW build process (Maintain Structure Functions).

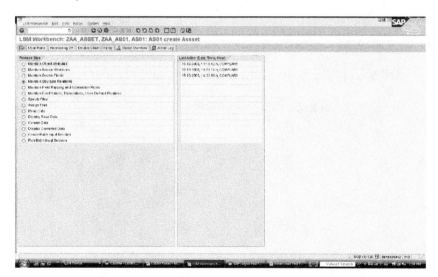

Create Mapping and Special Conversions

Move to the activity Maintain Field Mapping and

Conversion Rules. In this screen click the change icon

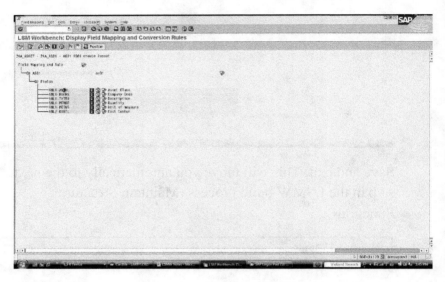

Highlight the field you want to map and click assign Source

Field by clicking on the blank page icon .

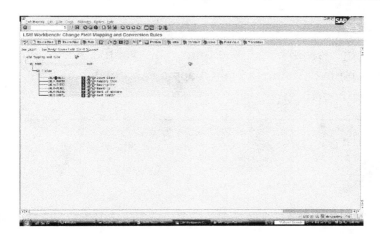

Attach each field from the load file to the above items as below. Ignore a message that the source field is longer than the target field. The screen below represents the view after everything has been assigned. Don't forget to save your work.

Assignment of Fixed Values

Most objects will be derived from your load file. For fixed values go into Maintain Field mapping and switch to change mode.

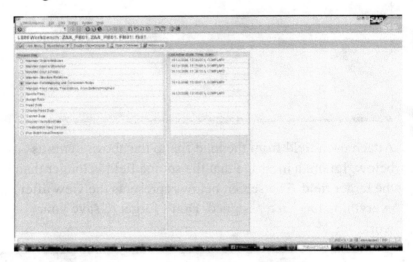

Click on the field that requires a fixed value and click on "Rule".

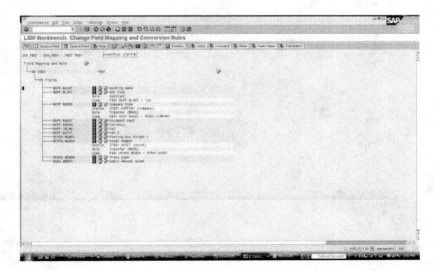

Choose "Constant".

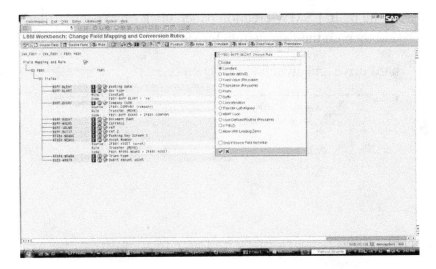

The screen looks like this after:

Save your work and return to the main LSMW creation panel.

Source File Specification

In the main LSMW creation panel, click on "Specify Files" and then on the first item below to access the file from your hard drive and switch to change mode  :

As sign your text tab delimited test file. After that is done enter any name in the second field.

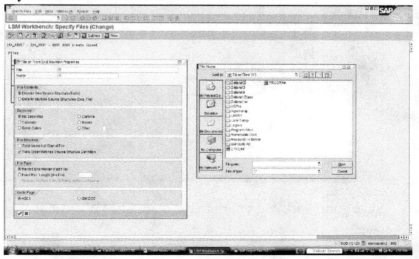

Change the settings to match those shown below
(Tabulator, Field Names at Start of File, Record End
Marker and ASCII):

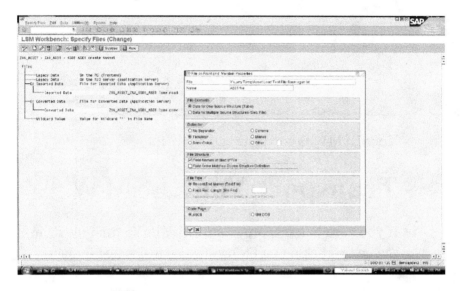

Click on Save ![save icon]. If the system issues an error message
that you exceeded the maximum length for either Imported
or Converted Data, shorten the length as required. Exit to
the main screen where you will automatically be positioned
in the next activity. You don't have to assign a file because
you only have one. Therefore, ignore "Assign Files."

Your LSMW is complete and ready for use.

Transport Your LSMW

If you need to transport your LSMW do so from the main screen by clicking on Extras<Generate Change Request.

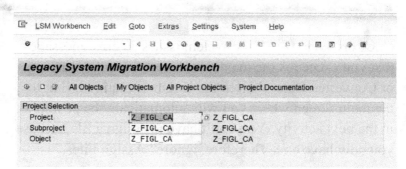

The following dialog box appears:

How to Create LSMW Programs

Enter the number of the change request you want to use or create a new one. Then follow the standard procedures in your organization.

Run Your LSMW Program

The remainder of the steps in the LSMW panel relate to the process of performing the load. At this point we will assume that you've tested your program and that if functions correctly. Regardless, the mechanics of testing for running a "live" LSMW program are identical. It begins with reading the data into your program, proceeds to converting so that it can be read by SAP, and the final step is executing the batch program to perform the data load. The last step moves you to the embedded transaction SM35.

Step One: Read Your Data

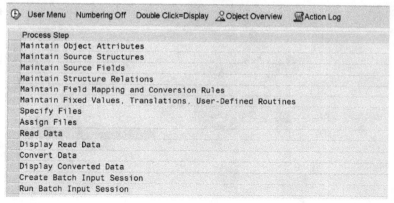

Note: This is a mandatory activity.

In this first step your text tab delimited file is read into the program. The name and location of the file was determined in the preceding section called "Source Specification", as was the format. Typically the file was first created in

Microsoft Excel and saved in the new format without

headers in the first row. Begin the step by clicking 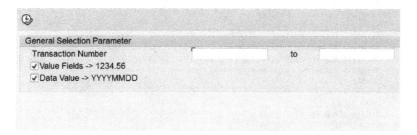.

Your results should look similar to this:

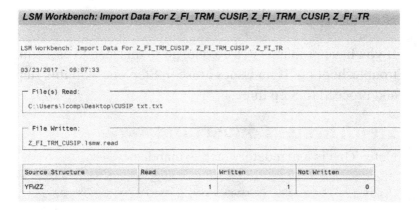

Back up and return to the main screen to continue.

Step Two: Display Read Data

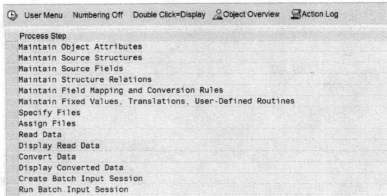

Note: this step is *optional*.

If you have problems in step one, go to this step to assist in troubleshooting. If no issues arose in Step one skip this step and proceed to Step three.

Step Three – Convert Data

Note: This is a mandatory step is mandatory.

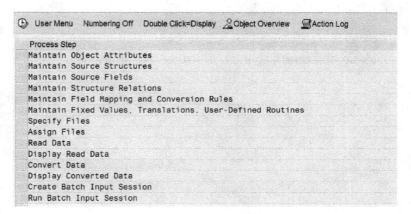

In this step you'll convert the data that you imported in step one, into code that SAP can read. Click on execute 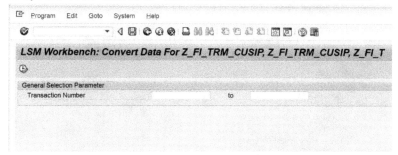.

Your results should look similar to this:

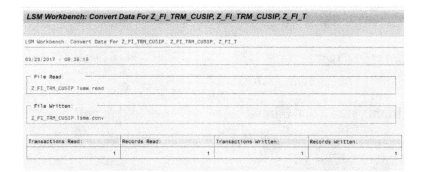

Step Four – Display Converted Data

Note: This is an *optional* step.

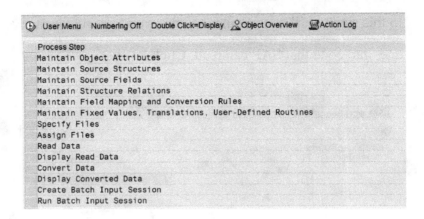

In this next step you'll display the data after it is converted into a form that SAP can upload. This step should only be executed if problems arose in the prior steps.

Step Five – Create Batch Input Session

Note: This is a *mandatory* step.

In this step a batch input session is created that will be executed in the next step. Click on the activity.

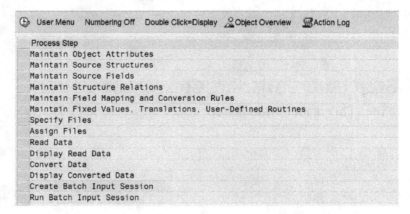

How to Create LSMW Programs

After entering the activity your screen will look similar to that shown below. Click on execute 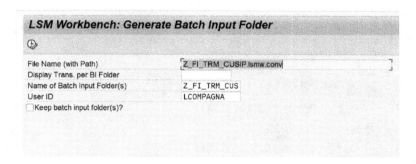.

If you are successful you will receive a message like this:

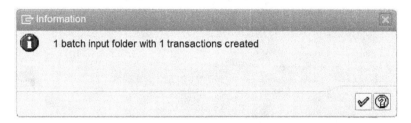

This message indicated that the batch input was created and is now resident in the SM35 screen. Proceed to Step Six.

Step Six- Initiate Load

The final LSMW step is to initiate the batch input session. After completing the preceding step you'll be move to the next activity.

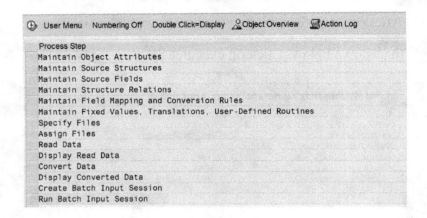

Click on the activity . Advanced users of SAP will recognize the screen that you are in. It is transaction code SM35, used by many other activities in SAP aside from LSMW.

Highlight the row that represents your batch input session. Since it has never been processed it will have a blank page

☐ icon in it. The number of items in your load are

indicated in the column shown with a 𝚺 above it. With the row still highlighted execute the process by clicking

⊕.

The following screen will pop up.

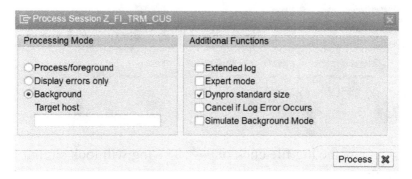

Click on the radio button for "Background" so that the process runs "behind the scenes" rather than in the foreground. Running in the foreground tends to be extremely time consuming. Error mode is less time consuming, and a useful analysis tool should your background job fail. Accept all other defaults. Once the settings are made, click on Process. The following message will pop up:

☑ 1 session(s) transferred to background processing

Unfortunately there is no refresh button, but you can simply hit "Enter" to refresh or back up to the main screen and re-enter. After an appropriate amount of time (depending on how much data was in your batch), reenter the SM35 screen.

If your job was successful it will no longer be in the queue (i.e. it will disappear from the SM35 screen) as shown in the following screen print:

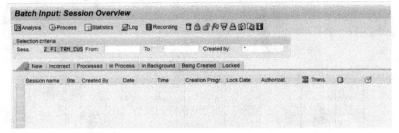

To view the log file click on . The log will look similar to this:

This log indicates success and the process is complete. If upon reentering the SM35 you find that your job is still there with records in the error column, you'll either have to repair the load file or fix the program. After fixing the issue, return to step one and repeat the process. If the job is still there with a indicator it is not finished processing. Exit the screen and return when the job is finished.

If your job completed successfully, congratulations! You are now an LSMW expert.

Tips and Tricks

Here are a few tips and tricks to help you create your own LSMW's:

- Remember to save frequently as you do steps!
- Keep your load file name short.
- Do a screen print of the file layout you create to help you prepare the load file.
- You can view all of your batch jobs in transaction code SM35. You can also view job logs for successful loads.
- Run the LSMW in background except to process errors.
- To prevent your LSMW program from overwriting fields that are already populated mark it as "only if Source Field Not initial" in the Change Field Mapping and Conversion Rules Screen as shown below:

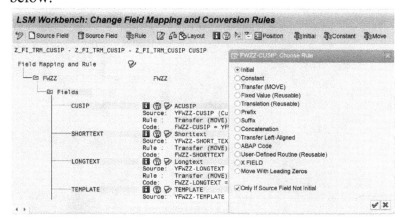

- Most data loads will not require any complex translation rules. If some are required the screen above is the tool to assist you.
- A constant can be inserted using the Field Mapping and Conversion rules as shown below:

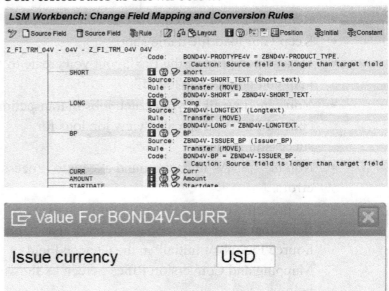

The Benefits

My hope is that by providing this tool to functional consultants and super users several benefits will be realized:

- Faster ability to react to situations that require the quick load of data.
- Eliminate the need to do a functional specification document (which is a communication tool between the functional resource and the technical resource).
- Reduce work by reducing direct data entry.

Conclusion

The Legacy System Migration Workbench is a great tool for loading data into SAP. As shown in this book, the tool does not require any direct coding to be effective and, with training, can be used by any functional person or super-user involved with SAP.

Finally, I leave you with a glossary of terms widely used in "SAPland" as well as a list of best practices for SAP implementations. I hope you find this document useful, and in particular find LSMW a powerful addition to your skill set.

Glossary of Terms

ABAP

ABAP is the programming language that the SAP Enterprise Central Component is written in. Those who code it are often called "ABAP'ers". Though SAP is an off the shelf system, there are still valid times when ABAP code must be added to the system by your own programmers. These include corrections that are sent by SAP, or available in through OSS notes (see glossary), and user exits.

Account Assignment Element

An account assignment element refers to the individual accounting assignments made on a given document. The elements may support financial, management, cost, fund, project, or any other type of accounting.

ASAP

ASAP, short for "accelerated SAP", is the traditional term for the SAP methodology project management methodology promoted by SAP since at least the mid 1990's. It has gone through variations and name changes over the years (e.g. "Value SAP"), but the term ASAP has been persistent among SAP professionals for many years.

Authorizations

Authorizations refer to the security profiles set up for each user that control what the users can create, modify and change. At their basic level authorizations control access to transaction codes. These transactions codes are then grouped into user roles which are then assigned to users.

Basis

Basis refers to the technical infrastructure of the SAP system. It includes the hardware, the software, and the connectivity of the system. It also refers to the technical settings of the system.

Basis Team

The Basis Team is responsible for the setup and maintenance of the hardware that the SAP software resides on, the application of the software to those boxes, and maintenance of those boxes. They are also responsible for the high level technical settings of the system.

Best Practice

The term best practice is term used quite broadly and often with no supporting evidence to show that a practice is in fact "best". Standard configurable SAP processes themselves are based on best practices. Methods considered "best" practices in this book (such as the prohibition against core modifications) are based on experience.

Big Bang

A big bang implementation is one where the full breadth of desired functionality is deployed. For example, it could include modules from the human resources, financials, and logistics areas, in addition to Customer Relationship Management and Business Intelligence. Aside from functionality, the term big bang could also be used to refer to the deployment of SAP to every business unit, and every geographic area (including all countries where the organization operates). See also "Phased".

Blueprint

A blue print is the primary design document for the "to-be" vision of the SAP system. Best practice is that it is based on requirements gleaned from a study of the subject organization's "as-is" process. It usually includes a discussion of gaps between requirements and SAP functionality and how they will be overcome.

Bolt-on

A "bolt-on" refers to a software package that is used to perform functions within SAP, but that is not part of the integrated SAP Enterprise Central Component system. Most often they are made by firms other than SAP, for example by one of the many sales and use tax package vendors (Vertex for example).

Bolt-ons can further be differentiated into those that were made by SAP, those that are certified by SAP, and those that are not certified by SAP. Obviously the non-certified software packages carry the most risk.

Box

A "Box" refers to a physical computer processing unit (CPU). From a configuration perspective the key consideration is that cross client configuration cannot jump from box to box, but this type of configuration can affect all of the clients within the box that it is housed in. Most configuration items are not cross client, so they only affect one particular client within the box.

Break Fix

After an SAP system has "gone live" and entered the support phase, a break-fix is any defect which is contrary to what the approved business blueprint and the functional specification documents say.

Business Process

A business process is a series of activities and SAP transaction codes that accomplish a business task. An end-to-end business practice, or a "cradle-to-grave" business process is one that traces the activities back to a trigger point and then carries the activities through a number of steps and a number of transaction codes (that often cross SAP modules), until it reaches a point where no further action is possible.

Certified

The term "Certified" can be used with reference to a person who has gone through one of the SAP academies for disciplines such as financials and controlling, human capital management, or public sector integration. It can also refer to complimentary third party software that has been "certified" for use with SAP.

Client

A client is an organizational unit where multiple company codes (an SAP organizational structure representing a distinct legal entity) are contained. Most configuration items do not cross clients, but there are some configuration activities that are cross client. As the name suggests, these are configuration changes that will affect all of the clients within a box.

Company Code

A company code is an SAP organizational structure representing a distinct legal entity. In the private sector these are usually incorporated entities that require a separate profit and loss statement and a separate balance sheet for statutory financial reporting.

Configuration

Configuration refers to the setting of flags, switches, and calculations in the SAP Implementation Guide (also called the IMG). These activities turn off and on standard SAP code. The processes that result are built on best industry practices.

See the Glossary entry for "Implementation Guide" to see a screen shot of it.

Controlling Module

The Controlling Module is the name given by SAP to the area that contains the functionality for management and cost accounting. It is abbreviated as CO, and contains its own ledger that operates parallel to the General Ledger of the Financial (FI) module.

Conversion

For our purposes this refers to the conversion of data from the legacy system to the New SAP system. The data could be master data, table data (for example choices in a configured list of responsible managers), and occasionally transaction data.

Core Modification (also known as a "Core Mod")

A core modification involves the insertion of ABAP code into a standard delivered SAP program, where no provision by SAP has been made to do so. For example, if transaction code FB01 is not a perfect fit for a business process, the insertion of code that enhances the functionality so that it more closely fits the business process is a called a core modification (assuming that SAP did not provide something like a user exit to facilitate this action). The inclusion of code in such a manner voids SAP's warranty and support for this specific transaction, so if there are problems with it you cannot rely on SAP for a fix.

Furthermore, future upgrades will overwrite your code with the original code, essentially breaking your process. When you upgrade, you will also be susceptible to changes that SAP has made to the process and the transaction code that may no longer be compatible with the enhancement your team made.

There are also changes that you can make in the configuration panel (i.e. the Implementation Guide or the IMG) that require a developer key. For our purposes we will call these "mini" core modifications. The fact that a developer key is required serves as a warning that a core modification may be in process.

The concept of a core modification does not include changes where SAP has designed a break point in their code where you can insert your own script. This is called a user exit, and it is not considered a core mod. The important distinction is that SAP has designed it so that you can include your own code in a user exit, and an upgrade will not over write this change.

In addition, the concept of a core mod does not encompass Z programs, Z tables, or Z transactions. The use of the "Z" prefix places the objects in the customer name space. By placing a Z object in the customer name space it will not be overwritten by an upgrade (as opposed to core modifications that will be overwritten). Thus if you have a developer copy the transaction code FB01 into a new transaction code ZFB01, and then copy the underlying program of this transaction SAPMF05A to ZSAPMF05A, any modifications you do to this Z program are not a core mod. Consequently the best practice should you absolutely need to make changes is to copy native SAP code and prefix it with a Z before you make your alterations. However, the new Z program is still susceptible to future changes to SAP and will not be supported by them. In this scenario you still have the original code of the original program intact and you can revert back to it at any time in the future.

Customer Message

A customer message denotes a message created by an SAP customer relating a possible product error in the software. Customer messages are created in the SAP online support system (which is referred to by the unofficial acronym OSS).

Cut-over

Cut-over refers to the time period when a number of steps, defined by the cut-over plan are initiated and carried out, eventually culminating in the official go-live day. The cut-over period usually extends for as long as a month before and a month after the go-live date.

Development (activity)

In SAP, the concept of development means any activity other than configuration (see definition earlier) that adds ABAP code to the SAP Enterprise Central Component system functions or creates code for the purposes of interfacing with the SAP Enterprise Central Component system.

Development (client)

Development in the context of the system landscape refers to the client where the initial configuration or ABAP development work is done. These clients reside on physical boxes that are different than those used for quality assurance or production purposes.

End-user

An end-user is a member of the business who uses SAP to conduct the day-to-day business of the organization.

End-user documentation

End-user documentation is an instruction manual intended to help the people who conduct the day-to-day business of the organization on the live SAP system.

Enhancement

The term enhancement is very general in nature and can refer to one of many possible changes to a live SAP system. The enhancement could be accomplished by making changes exclusively in the SAP Implementation Guide, through the use of ABAP programming, or by some other form of programming. Enhancements are very controlled, with their movement through the SAP landscape accomplished via transports that are moved by the Basis team.

Enterprise Central Component (ECC)

The Enterprise Central Component is the core of SAP's product offerings. It is the system SAP has built to handle most business processes within an organization. It comprises a multitude of modules in a highly integrated real-time system that can handle logistics, financials, and human resources. The "hallmark" of the SAP Enterprise

Central Component is the real-time integration between the modules within it.

Enterprise Resource Planning (ERP)

Enterprise resource planning, also known as ERP, is a blanket term for many different software packages that can run a wide variety of business processes. SAP is the leading vendor of ERP packages.

Functional

Functional refers to the business aspect of data flow within SAP. For example, the function of the system is to post vendor invoices. See also "technical".

Functional Specification

A functional specification documents the way a certain report, interface, conversion program, enhancement, form, or workflow is meant to work from a business perspective. Specifically it lists the business requirements. See also technical specification.

Functional Team

The term "functional team" refers to those people who are involved in how the standard SAP system functions from a business perspective. These people tend to be business people: people who were managers, business analysts, accountants, and engineers prior to working with SAP. They will usually have degrees in business, MBA's, degrees in disciplines like mechanical or civil engineering, or CPA's. Configuration of the standard SAP processes is undertaken by members of this team. This group works with the technical team by providing them functional expertise as they develop objects like interfaces.

Gap (functional)

In the world of SAP a functional gap indicates a functional deficit between what SAP standard configuration can support, and what the business requires in a certain business process. There are also other gaps within the framework of an SAP project such a technical and performance, but it is most commonly used with reference to business functionality.

General Ledger (GL)

General ledger is a common accounting term denoting the main ledger that statutory financial reports are derived from. In SAP this module is part of the financials module (SAP FI).

Golden Client

The golden client is the starting point for all system configuration that is meant to be migrated to the production client. It is located in a development box and contains only configuration and master data. Transaction data is not allowed in this client because it precludes certain kinds of configuration from being changed in the future (for example: the Funds Management Update Profile).

Go-live

The term go-live is the prevalent term in the world of SAP for the formal day that the system is viewed as being activated for general use in the business. Usually this means the first day that most end-users are able to log in and carry out their day-to-day duties. See also "cut-over".

Industry Solution

The SAP Enterprise Central Component is available in different industry solutions, for example: SAP Insurance, SAP Banking, SAP Public Sector Management, and SAP Utilities. Each industry solution has slight variations to make SAP more applicable to the industry. For example: the utilities version has a different nomenclature for SAP Plant Maintenance (PM) objects and uses a unique billing and invoicing solution (ISU Billing and ISU invoicing), whereas the public sector solution has a unique tool called FMDerive to aid in its unique fund accounting and budget requirements.

Below is a partial list of SAP Industry Solutions:

Industry Solutions of SAP	
Aerospace & Defense	Life Sciences
Automotive	Logistics Service Prod.
Banking	Media
Chemicals	Mining
Consumer Products	Oil & Gas
Defense & Security	Pharmaceuticals
Healthcare	Postal Services
Higher Education	Professional Services
Industrial Machinery	Railways
Insurance	Telecommunications

Implementation

For our purposes, an implementation refers to the initial installation of SAP, or part of SAP. A Greenfield implementation refers to an implementation where no SAP system has previously existed.

Implementation Guide (IMG)

The Implementation Guide (abbreviated to IMG) is the part of SAP where configuration is performed. In the IMG, all of the standard SAP functionality can be turned on, turned off, and modified to the extent that standard SAP allows. Tables used for drop down menus can also be populated, as can calculations. The IMG can be accessed through the transaction code SPRO.

Because of the power of the IMG, it is carefully controlled. It cannot be accessed at all in any client by most users. Configuration personnel have access to it the development client, but have read-only access in the quality assurance and production environments.

This is what the implementation guide looks like:

Implementation Partner

An organization that is intent on implementing SAP, or any other large project involving SAP, will usually hire an implementation partner. The "implementation partner" refers to a firm that has expertise in SAP (and business transformation in general) that will help the business achieve the objectives of the project. Generally speaking the implementation partner will also assist the business in avoiding unnecessary risk when implementing the software. Another term for implementation partner is software integrator or systems integrator.

Instance

Sometimes different SAP landscapes (see definition) are required to support different geographic regions (for example one in Asia, one in North America) or when multiple industry solutions are required for one organization (for example: an organization that needs to run the SAP utilities solution and the SAP public sector management version for different aspects of their business.

Integration

Integration refers to data flow between modules. SAP is referred to as integrated because data entered once into the system flows seamlessly between modules in real-time.

Integration Test

Integration testing refers to the testing of an end to end business process (also known as cradle to grave testing). The trigger for the beginning of a process is identified and that is where the test starts. The process continues from SAP module to SAP module until it is complete. The process tends to be quite formal with a script that is usually based on real life scenarios in the organization.

Interface

A program built to handle the data flow between the core SAP Enterprise Central Component program and external programs. Usually these external programs are not manufactured by SAP.

Landscape

In the world of SAP, a landscape refers to a complete infrastructure that supports separate development, testing (staging), and production boxes (see "box"). This three tiered landscape is considered a minimum, there are often more environments than this at an SAP installation site.

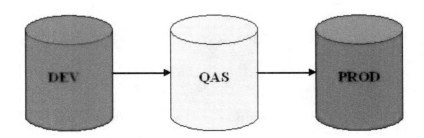

Legacy Systems Migration Workbench (LSMW)

The Legacy Systems Migration Workbench is a tool provided in the standard SAP Enterprise Central Component for converting data into SAP.

Lessons Learned Session

"Lessons Learned" workshops are a series of meetings conducted in the interest of continuous improvement to improve the implementation process by examining what worked and what did not work. From a legal perspective, such a session will be closely examined should litigation arise down the road (refer to the section on litigation proofing for more information).

> **"I have not failed, I've just found 10,000 ways that won't work"**
>
> — Thomas Edison

Live

In the SAP world, a "Live" system is one where the productive system is in general business use. Such a state follows the day of "Go-live".

"Mini" Mods

For our purposes a modification to SAP code that is facilitated by SAP itself is what some professionals in the industry call a mini modification, or a "mini-mod" for short.

Included in this definition of mini mods are user exits, customer includes, s-mods, and c-mods. An example of such a change to SAP is the change of the label for the field "Cost Center" to "Department".

There are also changes that you can make in the configuration panel (i.e. the IMG) that require a developer key. For our purposes we will call these "mini" core mods as well.

Extending our definition, there are items in the configuration panel (i.e. IMG) that SAP strongly recommends that you do not change, however these items do not require a developer key to alter. Unfortunately, there are no system controls to prevent such changes by your configuration personnel.

Mini mods, like core mods, are susceptible to being overwritten in an upgrade (though much less so). The Basis team can run job prior to an upgrade which shows all such objects contained in your SAP system.

Though these changes are minor compared to a true core mod, it is still recommended that they be avoided because they tend to cause problems later on during the support phase of the project, especially during upgrades.

Module

The SAP Enterprise Central Component is divided into a series of modules that are specifically designed for a general function. For example, management and cost accounting are handled by the Controlling module, also abbreviated to CO. The Materials Management module, also called MM, is designed to handle the logistics of physical materials processing.

When a company buys the SAP Enterprise Central Component, they receive software that has all of these modules in it. None of them are active until the configuration teams activates them, but they are all present Thus, an organization may be running on SAP, but they do not realize the code for an out of scope module like Quality Management (QM) is already in their productive system lying dormant.

Also, generally speaking, all of these modules are seamlessly integrated in real time. If you enter data in one module, it is passed on to all subsequent modules and never needs to be entered again. This powerful integration is the hallmark of SAP.

There are a few modules that are not integrated real time to the general ledger, such as contract accounting (FICA), but they are by far in the minority.

OSS (Online Support System)

The term "OSS" is the informal term used by people involved with implementing and supporting SAP to refer to the system provided by SAP to research issues that often cannot be resolved through configuration or user training. The acronym OSS has survived from a time when SAP's help system was called the "online support system". The same system has since gone through several name changes.

Often the OSS system provides corrections that can be applied to your system to resolve the issue. In order to access the OSS system your BASIS administrator must create an ID for you to use that requires a password.

Using the OSS system you can also set up access for SAP to review the issue in your system and give you an opinion. This will sometimes result in SAP logging into your system and directly fixing the problem, or developing a fix specifically to resolve the situation.

OSS Note

An OSS note is a document found in SAP`s online support system repository that contains information that can be used to resolve a problem in its software. Many OSS notes contain Corrections, which contain code that can be used to patch the system, while other notes contain programs that can fix the problem. Some OSS notes contain recommendations on how to solve the problem without the use of additional code or programs.

Below is a sample of what the SAP OSS database looks like as at the time of writing. (Courtesy of SAP AG)

Package Slam

A package slam is a somewhat derogatory term used by SAP professionals to denote an SAP implementation where short cuts from best practice are used to compress the timeline of the project. Short cuts can include: no blueprint or a blue print without a review of the as-is, functional or technical specification documents are skipped, or less (or no) integration and or user acceptance testing cycles. Package slams are extremely risky for both the business and the implementation partner. A package slam is often motivated by onerous obligations in a contract.

Phased Approach

A phased approach attempts to break up what would be much larger SAP project (with a much bigger scope) into a series of smaller projects with a tighter scope. Such an approach presents less risk to the business.

Production

Production refers to the actual client that the organization performs its day-to-day business on. It is a carefully controlled environment and one where configuration is not possible.

Project Management Office (PMO)

The project management office is as general term for the team in charge of the general management of an SAP project. It includes the project directors, project managers, and administrative staff.

Prototype

A prototype is a configured SAP demonstration system usually created in a sandbox environment for the purposes of presenting the business with a preliminary view of the proposed SAP solution. It is sometimes called a "straw man".

Quality Assurance Client

The quality assurance client (also known as QA) is the client where integration testing and user acceptance testing are performed. This client always resides on a physical box different than the boxes where the development and productive instances occur.

Real Time

In system integration the term "real time" refers to integration between modules that does not require a batch program to be run. In real time integration, data passes from one module to another immediately. In particular, accounting data from sub-ledgers like accounts payable are summarized and sent over to the general ledger immediately. For example, if you post a document in the accounts payable module and look at the general ledger for the account that was credited you will immediately see the impact.

Realization

The aspect of an SAP project concerned with actually building the SAP solution, either through the use of the configuration panel (the IMG), or through development.

Reconciliation

The term reconciliation is a general accounting term. It refers to the activity of proving that a financial balance is correct using various accounting methods. One of the best known reconciliation is that of the bank account. The general ledger bank account balance is simply compared to the statement produced by the bank. An itemized statement accounting for differences between the two balances is used to prove the integrity of the general ledger account.

Refresh

A refresh refers to the copying of data and configuration usually from the Production client to another client, often the quality assurance client or a sandbox.

Regression Test

A test performed to assure that functionality that had previously performed satisfactorily still functions correctly after a change has been put through that could have negatively affected it.

Re-implementation

Occasionally a new SAP implementation replaces a preexisting SAP implementation in its entirety. In such an implementation the old SAP system is treated like a legacy system and all other phases of a normal SAP green field implementation are carried out. There are several reasons to do a re-implementation: the prior implementation may have been a poor one with the modules not being used in the way they were meant. Another reason is that there may have been a number of core modifications done to the old system that have made upgrading to the latest version of SAP impossible.

The term can also be used for the re-deployment of a module or several modules to replace the exact same modules in an existing SAP system. In this case the module or modules are "re-imagined" in a new business blueprinting phase and the system is reconfigured according to the new design. There are many situations where a reimplementation of a module(s) may be required:

it may have been a bad implementation with the modules not being used in the way they were intended, or a new factor may have emerged that may have necessitated a complete overhaul of the way the module is used (for example a change to International Financial Reporting Standards).

Release Notes

SAP's Release Notes highlight the differences between a previous version and the one that these notes document. They can be found in SAP's service portal.

Request for Proposal (RFP)

An invitation sent by an organization to a select group of vendors inviting them to put forth a proposal (for SAP integration services for example).

Requirements

The term "requirements" refers to the business needs of an organization that underlie certain functions and processes. For example, if an organization is utilizing International Financial Reporting Standards then one of the business requirements of the SAP Asset Accounting module is that it carries a book of depreciation that is in accordance with those standards.

Requirements Traceability Matrix

A requirements traceability matrix is a document that lists every business requirement discussed in the business blueprint and then traces the requirements through each configuration and testing phase so that there is visibility as to the status of the requirements being satisfied. The requirements traceability matrix can also be used to indicate the status of the project as a whole.

RICEFW

The acronym RICEFW refers to the combined development objects of Reports, Interfaces, Enhancements, Forms, and Workflow.

Scope

The scope of an SAP project refers to the breadth of functionality to be deployed, the modules to be deployed, the interfaces to be deployed, and sometimes the custom development that will be generated from a project.

Scope Creep

Scope creep refers to an increase in scope such that the scope is now bigger than it was originally envisioned.

Script

A script is a testing document that is used in various tests, especially integration and user acceptance. It is usually scenario based in that it incorporates a real life trigger to a chain of business transactions and processes, and follows them right through to the last possible event in the chain.

Security

The term "security", when used in an SAP context, has a different meaning than the usual information technology definition. Security for SAP refers to the authorization schemes that are managed by the security team. The authorizations determine who can do what in the SAP system. It does not refer to security against threats such as that posed by a virus.

Solution

Out of a list of alternatives, a solution is the recommended course of action to solve an issue.

Solution Manager

The Solution Manager system is a stand-alone product that SAP has designed for use with its software offerings. Solution Manager can be used many different ways. Often it is used as a document repository for things such as blueprints, functional specification documents, technical documents, landscape diagrams, and any other document pertaining to SAP. It can also be used as a work management system (with tickets).

Scope

Scope refers to the list of functionality and changes that are within the mandate of the team to work on and transform.

Standard SAP

The term "standard SAP" refers to functionality in the SAP Enterprise Central Component that can be achieved through configuration alone. The term can be loosely applied to SAP functionality that required user exits to achieve as well. The term does not include functionality achieved by means of core modifications to SAP's code, solutions that use Z-programs, or solutions that use Z-tables.

Statement of Work

A statement of work is a document that lists the details of an engagement including the deliverables, timeline, and scope. It is often a binding contractual agreement that can be appended to a general contract.

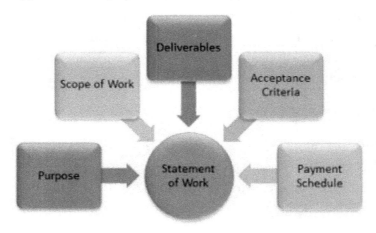

Steering Committee

A steering committee is a group composed of senior executives from the business and its implementation partner, as well as the leaders of the project itself. The project sponsor must always be part of the committee.

Stress Test

A stress test is one that is designed to emulate the actions of many processes being run simultaneously by many users. It is usually conducted by the Basis team.

String Test

A string test refers to a string of transaction codes involved in a process that are used in sequence to test a process. It is more comprehensive than a unit test, but less comprehensive than an integration test. During an implementation the integration test will encompass all transaction codes, and thus they also constitute a string test.

Support

Support refers to a period after the SAP system or change has gone live when the team is in "break/fix" mode addressing any reported defects in the system. Many of the perceived defects tend to be training issues.

Support Pack

A support pack consists of multiple OSS bug fixes that are applied all at once to an SAP system. It is likened to a mini-upgrade, but does not encompass any new functionality.

System Integration – see Integration

System Integrator – see Implementation partner

Technical

In general terms the word "technical" in an SAP context means any functionality attained by a means other than configuration via the Implementation Guide.

Technical Specification Document

Usually called a tech spec, the technical specification document outlines the programming logic necessary for the requirements of a functional specification document to be realized.

Technical Team

The technical team consists mostly of programmers who take care of the actual coding of ABAP programs and other types of programs. They build interfaces, code ABAP enhancements, and carry out things like user exits. They work closely with the members of the functional team.

Technical Upgrade

A technical upgrade refers to the movement of an SAP system to a higher version without activating any of the new functionality available in that version.

Testing Team

A team charged with carrying out integration testing, string, and regression testing. If the team is composed of end-users they will be charged with carrying out user acceptance testing (UAT) as well. However, the team that performs UAT should not be the same as the team that carries out any other form of testing. Unit testing is outside the scope of testing for either team as it is performed by the people who made the change.

Timeline

A timeline refers to the duration of a project. A typical timeline of a large SAP project using the ASAP methodology is nine to 12 months.

Transaction Code

A transaction code is a short cut for executing a function in SAP. For example, typing in transaction code FB01 will lead you to the screen for entering a general journal entry into the general ledger without having to go through the menu system.

Transport

Transports are the mechanism, administrated by the Basis members of your SAP team, by which configuration and development changes are moved between the development clients and the quality assurance clients (also known as staging) , and once they are successfully tested to the live production client.

Unit Testing

A "unit test" refers to testing within a module, often within a single transaction of that module. This type of testing tends to be informal and conducted by the person who configured or developed the change.

Upgrade

An upgrade refers to the process of elevating the version level of an SAP system to a version higher than the existing one. Upgrades do not have to be sequential. For example, an organization currently on version 4.7 can upgrade directly to the latest version of SAP without having to upgrade to the versions between it and the latest version.

User Acceptance Test (UAT)

A user acceptance test is a test performed by the users to give them an opportunity to approve a change prior to it being moved to the production client. It is usually performed in a quality assurance client (sometimes called a staging client). In an implementation the user acceptance test usually follows the same scripts as those used for integration testing. After the system is live the user acceptance test will resemble more of a unit test or a string test. The bigger the impact of change, the more comprehensive the testing and the closer it gets to an end-to-end integration test.

User Exit

A user exit refers to a change to a standard SAP program's code where SAP has provided an insertion point so that an ABAP developer from the business can insert their own code. This is called a user exit, and it is not considered a core modification to the system. The important distinction is that SAP has designed it so that your team to include its own programming logic. An upgrade will not overwrite this work.

Despite this type of change being specifically designed for your team to insert its own code it is still ABAP development that will require a Functional Specification document as well as a Technical Specification document. It requires a considerable amount of work (relative to configuration) and should be avoided if possible.

Vanilla SAP

A "vanilla SAP" project refers to the implementation of an SAP system without the use of any core modifications to its code. A more extreme definition of this would also include that a vanilla SAP system has no Z-tables and no Z-programs.

Volume Test

A volume test is one that is designed to emulate the actions of many processes being run simultaneously by many users. It is usually conducted by the Basis team.

War Room

In SAP project terms a "war room" refers to a large space housing the majority of the SAP project team. Such a room has no walls. This open environment promotes quick communication between team members, and allows others on the team to hear conversations that the speakers may not think are relevant to them, but are.

Work Breakdown Structure Element

A work breakdown structure element in the SAP Project Systems module is a cost collector that reflects a logical piece of work on a project. It is also a common term utilized in project management outside of SAP circles.

Z-Objects

In SAP a "Z object" is any programming that has a Z prefix. It can be a program, table, or transaction. The significance of the Z is that it places the programming in the SAP customer name space protecting it from being overwritten by upgrades.

Z-Programs, Z-Tables, and Z-Transactions

The use of the "Z" prefix places the objects in the customer name space. Such objects will not be overwritten by an upgrade. Thus if you have a developer copy the transaction code FB01 into a new transaction code ZFB01, and then copy the underlying program of this transaction SAPMF05A to ZSAPMF05A, any modifications you do to this Z program are not a core modification. Consequently the best practice should you absolutely need to make changes is to copy native SAP code and prefix it with a Z before you make your alterations. However, the new Z program is still susceptible to future changes to SAP and will not be supported by them. In this scenario you still have the original code of the original program intact and you can revert back to it at any time in the future.

Of these objects the Z transaction is the lowest risk and requires the least amount of labor to develop. On the other hand Z-programs and Z-tables involve considerable time to develop and can materially change the performance of SAP.

In an extreme example of the use Z programs, I once had a client that had essentially designed their own module for management accounting purposes through the extensive use of Z programs and Z tables. These Z program and tables were extremely buggy. They also ignored the fact that SAP already had a well established module for management accounting called the Controlling module (CO) that incorporates best practices. The poorly performing custom module based on Z programs and tables had to be deactivated, and the CO module implemented in its place.

Because of examples such as the above I recommend that Z programs and Z tables be avoided in your SAP project, and be considered comparable to core modifications.

Appendix: Best Practices Summary

This is a summary of the best practices described in the book "SAP Best Practices" by Lawrence Compagna, CPA:

1. Do not allow any core modifications to SAP code.
2. Any development in SAP should be prefixed with either a "z" or a "y" to place it in the customer name space.
3. Standard SAP should be an 80% fit for your business processes.
4. A technical upgrade should precede a functional one.
5. The phased project approach is the best practice (versus a "big bang").
6. An SAP project must never exceed one year in duration.
7. Observe the one to one rule: every external consulting staff member is matched to one from the business.
8. The as-is state must be studied to derive the true business requirements.
9. Integration and user acceptance testing must be scenario based.
10. A string test should precede the integration test.
11. The financial data conversion should be based on loading the trial balance after it has been closed to retained earnings.

12. When financial data is involved go-live must be the first day of the fiscal year.
13. Training, security, and user acceptance testing should be linked.
14. Configuration should be performed by the business, not its consultants.
15. Financial reconciliations by qualified accountants must be part of testing.
16. Configuration should only be possible in development clients. Production, test, and quality assurance clients must always be locked.
17. Observe the "vanilla" SAP philosophy. Business processes must be changed to fit into those supported in standard SAP.
18. "As at" balances should be loaded into SAP. Transactional data should not be.
19. Functional people must do their own data conversions using LSMW (see Appendix for "how to guide").
20. Custom applications should not be in sap (i.e. those with containing data entry points and multiple tables).
21. Custom reports should not be in the first phase of an SAP project. They should be in later ones.
22. The first phase rolls out established sap modules that are a good fit for the business.
23. Four best practices for go live date:

- In a live SAP system non-fiscal year dependent changes should not go-live at the end of the fiscal year.

- Fiscal year dependent changes *should* go live at the beginning of a fiscal year.
- For payroll related changes go live on a non-pay week between April and November.
- Go live on a holiday weekend (if possible).

24. Historical data must not be loaded.
25. Cut an interface from scope if it won't cause an additional SAP module to be implemented.
26. Cut and SAP module from scope if it won't necessitate the build of an interface.
27. If financial processes are involved the SAP General Ledger must always be in scope.
28. Payroll projects should be done on their own.
29. Keep the team size lean.
30. For projects extending over multiple jurisdictions (country or county for example) use a template approach. Roll the template out over time.
31. Perform due diligence early in the project to determine the degree of fit between as-is business processes and those in SAP.
32. When a process is a bad fit for SAP either build an interface to a program that better satisfies he requirements or push it out of scope.
33. Mini-modifications, Z-programs, and Z-tables should not be included in the initial scope of a project. Core modifications should never be part of it.
34. Each module has an expert advising on its implementation.

35. Create a resource loaded project plan early in the first phase of the project.
36. The Project plan is initially created top-down, refined with bottom up participation, and controlled centrally.
37. Project managers must vigilantly reduce scope.
38. Blueprint documents must show a clear relationship between the as-is and the requirements.
39. A "c level" project sponsor must adamantly demand only standard configurable SAP processes be employed.
40. Prototyping should begin in the blueprint phase.
41. All large SAP projects must have a change management team.
42. All development requires senior management approval.
43. Halt the project until Blue Prints are signed off.
44. Use a requirements traceability matrix to track business requirements to their finish.
45. Use on-site resources, not offshore.
46. Safeguard the integrity of the golden client. No transactional data is allowed.
47. Unit testing must be informal.
48. Configuration must be done by a member of the organization implementing SAP with their expert advisor looking over their shoulder.
49. Use transaction code SCC1 to support the unit test process.
50. All transaction codes must be contained within both integration and user acceptance tests.

51. Signatures on the user acceptance test are required for every script before the project can progress from the realization phase to the project preparation phase

52. The realization phase should have the longest duration.

53. Do not go live if there are significant "show-stopper" issues.

54. When possible close all financial open items, for example payables.

55. At the end of the project set the SAP productive indicators

56. Have plans for the following: risk management, change management, and training.

57. Have published policies for key items like core modifications.

58. The security team must piggy back on the work of the training team to ensure that only those who have been trained have access to that part of the SAP system

59. Four day onsite schedule for travelers, ideally Tuesday to Friday.

60. Subject all functional and technical specification documents to a peer review.

61. Consulting module leads must fit this profile: they are certified by SAP, have participated in multiple go-lives, have ten or more years of experience, have the right academic background, and were experts in the subject area prior to SAP. They are also fluent in the language of the project.

62. The business must have the right to interview and refuse the resources the consulting firm wishes to place on the project.
63. Organizations implementing SAP must engage an SAP quality assurance consultant to assess the consulting firm's quality of work.
64. Use Dice.com to supplement your staff.
65. Incubate new talent as you implement.
66. The authors of configuration meant for production must be from the business. They must also document the configuration as they perform it.
67. Only consulting leads have the ability to release transports.
68. Maintain a skill set risk profile and plan.
69. The best practices for project location and conditions:

- The setting should be a "war room" environment consisting of a big open area suitable for the entire team at its maximum size.

- The entire on site team must be housed there, and it should be near the project sponsor and other key external people.

- The environment should be healthy, with access to flu shots, fitness facilities, coffee, and food.

70. Because it lowers travel costs and benefits staff retention every SAP project must have a limited work from home policy.
71. Use Skype and other video conferencing technologies to aid the offsite worker.

72. The project must consist of the right mix of expert, senior, junior, administrative, and clerical personnel. Senior people costing the project hundreds of dollars per hour shouldn't be doing clerical work.

73. In project preparation everyone on the team should have a functional background. A Basis person is the first technical member on-boarded.

74. Development people are not required on the project team until sometime during the second phase (blueprinting).

75. The time and materials type of contract is best for both the business and the consulting firm.

76. For external consulting companies susceptible to litigation: lessons learned workshops are a bad practice, not a best practice.

77. For external consulting companies susceptible to litigation: if there are major issues do not communicate about them in writing and avoid taking notes.

78. For external consulting companies susceptible to litigation: incorporate "litigation proofing" sessions into your routine team meetings.

79. Deviations from standard configurable SAP settings must require sign-off from both the project sponsor and the senior manager of the implementation partner.

80. Contract stipulates that only "vanilla" SAP will be implemented.

81. Contract stipulates that network and data center environments are stable during the SAP project. Events such as data center moves are not permitted.

82. The best practice for SAP reports or programs that you wish to modify is to copy the standard into a "Z" version and attach a "Z" transaction code to it

83. Transactional data is not permitted in the golden configuration client.

84. To prevent the posting of transactions in the golden client close all periods in the Finance module (transaction code OB52), Controlling (transaction OKP1), and Materials Management (MMPV).

85. Transaction code SCC1 must be used to keep the unit test client in sync with the golden client; have team leads sign off that all transports have been "SCC1'd" into the unit test client: have the Basis team report monthly on transports that are in the golden client but not in the unit test client; perform a scheduled year-end annually in the unit test client.

86. The user acceptance test (UAT) is the key risk control device for the external consulting firm.

87. Each defect uncovered during integration or user acceptance testing must have a regression test plan. The plan must carry an assessment of the materiality of the change (high, medium, low), as well as one concerning its impact on other downstream modules.

88. Smart numbering should not be used in SAP.

89. Only security by transaction code is encompassed in the plan. Explicitly spell out in the contract and other formal project documents that no other types

of SAP security will be employed. (E.g. There will be no security by document type, cost center, or general ledger account.)

90. The project team must not be burdened with undue security restraints.

91. Have a documented contingency plan to handle unforeseen issues. It should demonstrate that the initiative has sufficient budget, slack, redundant resources in key positions, and a plan to handle turnover.

About the Author

Lawrence Compagna has provided SAP consulting services for two decades. He is a CPA who was SAP Academy Certified as an SAP Consultant in 1998 and received a certificate in SAP's ASAP Project Management methodology in 2001. In the SAP ERP sphere he has been a management consultant, a systems integrator, an advisor, a solution architect, an expert witness in SAP related litigation, and a project manager. He has also served as the advisor to the chief operating officer of one of the world's largest SAP integrators performing "best practice" audits of their implementations. He has consulted to a variety of industries including manufacturing, telecommunications, utilities, professional services, and public sector. His past clients include: Mercedes Benz, the US Army, Compaq Computers (now HP), Deloitte Consulting, the State of California (Judicial), and the United Nations.

Mr. Compagna's successful leadership over the merger of two NASDAQ traded telecommunications companies on the SAP platform is among his career highlights.

Visit the author's website at: Compagna.xyz

Facebook page at: fb.me/LawrenceCompagna